The Ripple Effect of Gun Violence

A Worldwide Crisis

By

Wayne Anderson

Table Of Contents:

Dedication

First, let me start off by saying, there are no words that I could write or say to tell you how sorry I am for your loss. Please know that globally you are in many thoughts and prayers. This book has been written and inspired by the death of six-year-old King Carter. I could only imagine at that time if that were my son, and it touched my heart as if that were my very own.

As such a time as now, the ripple effect of gun violence continues rapidly with in our communities, so close that this time killing one of my three-year-old niece's mother and grazing her. A scar she will never forget. To everyone affected, especially the parents and children of those slain, this book is written and released in honor and dedication to your loved ones, that has been victims of Gun Violence. Gun violence has been a nationwide issue in America for over a decade.

It saddens me to know from the days of old to the present America have upgraded greatly on gun power and the availability to purchase military-style guns, which increases the chances of the wrong hands being able to get weapons that they are able to continue to cause a ripple effect of Gun Violence. Gun violence has claimed so many innocent lives and it must stop. Gun Violence has increased so rapidly, creating a sense of being the norm around the world, that people have become immune to it symptoms and when they hear of the gun violence it brings no effect as if this is really a normal thing to happen.

IN LOVING

memory

In honor of everyone that is listed, unknown by me and unliste

IN LOVING

memory

FATAL SHOOTINGS IN MIAMI,FLORIDA

Real people, not just statistics.

AMERICANS KILLED WITH GUNS
Around the world, A Worldwide Crisis

As of June 23, 2021

82,298 Gun violence victims and counting

National Gun Violence Memorial (gunmemorial.org)

About 64% of gun deaths were the results of homicide. Nearly nine out of 10 people killed by gun violence were men, and the highest number of deaths were people between 20 and 24 years old.

worldpopulationreview.com

Gun violence in the U.S results in More than 39,000 deaths annually. In 2020, there were 19,000 deaths linked to firearms related incidents and shootings. This was the highest death toll rate in 20 years (Bates, 2020). This number includes both accidental and homicidal deaths and does not include suicides (Baates, 2020). According to the Gun Violence Archives so far this year there have been 5,605 deaths attributed to gun violence, not including suicide (2021). Facts about Gun Violence in the U.S

- Gun Violence is the leading cause of premature death in the U.S (APHA, 2021).
- Increasing the number of deaths and injuries resulting from gun violence is a major public health concern (APHA, 2021).
- Requires evidence-based multidimensional solutions (APHA,2021).
- Of all guns related death in just about two dozen high income countries 82% take place in the U.S (APHA, 2021).
- Among citizens between ages 15-24, homicide is the fourth leading cause of death in white, second for Hispanics and first in non-Hispanic blacks (APHA, 2021).
- Gun violence cost the U.S $280billionannually (APHA,2021

IN LOVING

memory

Johnnie Stephen
Dixson, Jr.
Jun 8, 2021

Lucretia Danielle
Braithwaite
Jun 8, 2021

Jaheim Ziegler
Jun 6, 2021

Tyleisha Taylor
Jun 6, 2021

William Everett Jr
Jun 6, 2021

Jason Campbell
Jun 1, 2021

Edson Dorce
May 31, 2021

Clayton Dillard, III
May 30, 2021

Desmond Owens
May 30, 2021

Shaniqua Lechelle
Peterson
May 30, 2021

Johnny A. Collins, II
May 8, 2021

Maame Adwoa Amuah
May 6, 2021

LeShonte'
Ar'Darsheney Jones
May 3, 2021

Dominique Belleville
Apr 18, 2021

Clinton Young
Apr 7, 2021

Stephanie Lacrete
Mar 27, 2021

Ivan "Sito" Horta
Mar 9, 2021

Carlton Tillman
Mar 6, 2021

Alexander Garrido
Feb 17, 2021

Diana Ceballos
Feb 17, 2021

Nimikae Clarke
Feb 13, 2021

Dawann N. Graham
Feb 5, 2021

Zariya Williams
Feb 5, 2021

Michael Anthony
Mackey, Jr.
Jan 19, 2021

Chassidy "Tik Tok
Princess" Saunders
Jan 16, 2021

Aaron Nelson
Swerdloff
Jan 13, 2021

Ivan Mir Brodsky
Dec 21, 2020

Kwakutl Belizaire
Dec 20, 2020

Raul Amor
Nov 28, 2020

Kerry Jacques
Nov 5, 2020

Donovan Perez
Nov 1, 2020

IN LOVING

memory

Timothy King
Oct 28, 2020

Anton Walker
Oct 22, 2020

Brandon Bennett
Oct 21, 2020

Matthew Brown
Sep 26, 2020

Corey Smith
Sep 21, 2020

Pastor Gregory Boyd
Sep 10, 2020

Jay J. Cephus
Aug 28, 2020

Jose Luis Contreras
Carmona
Aug 27, 2020

Jefferey Dumersaint
Aug 17, 2020

Arrington L Veargis Jr
Aug 15, 2020

Demetrius D Campbell
Aug 15, 2020

Alana Washington
Jul 25, 2020
Khadijah Robinson
Jun 21, 2020

Precious Anne
Paraison
Jun 18, 2020

Garry Laguerre
Jun 16, 2020

Arya Gray
May 12, 2020

Miriame Pierre
May 11, 2020

Kristopher Vega
May 5, 2020

Andrea Camps
Lacayo
Apr 7, 2020

Barbaro Lara
Feb 8, 2020

Jose Trimaine Jose
Feb 7, 2020

Arlety Garcia
Jan 28, 2020

Isabela Valdes
Jan 28, 2020

Lina Gonzalez
Jan 28, 2020

Ivelisse Alvarado
Sanchez
Jan 26, 2020

Nalton Johnson Jr
Jan 17, 2020

Silvio Horta
Jan 7, 2020

Melissa Gonzalez
Jan 3, 2020

Terrance Stevenson
Jan 3, 2020

Donna D Edwards
Dec 29, 2019

Rony Dassas
Dec 27, 2019

Dennis McGhee
Dec 24, 2019

IN LOVING

memory

Carlos Martinez Jr Dec 21, 2019	Male, age 30 Aug 18, 2019	Gabriela "Gabi" Aldana May 24, 2019
Julia Caridad Martinez Dec 21, 2019	Alexis Palencia Aug 14, 2019	Jonathan Varela May 12, 2019
Jamal Keyshawn Pieze Nov 17, 2019	Christopher Tassy Aug 11, 2019	Reginald Joseph May 7, 2019
Daniel Mackey Nov 5, 2019	Jorge C Chacon Arza Aug 2, 2019	Courtney Forbes May 5, 2019
Deandre Barnes Oct 22, 2019	Kiki Fantroy Jul 31, 2019	Joanna Telusme Apr 14, 2019
Angel Cueli Oct 19, 2019	Winnie Mendoza Jul 26, 2019	Stephanie Telusme Apr 14, 2019
Eduardo Gonzalez Oct 9, 2019	Troy Wilson Jul 22, 2019	Edward Nellicliff Apr 6, 2019
Shanica Harris Sep 28, 2019	Annie Gentles Jul 14, 2019	Jesse Henry Mar 31, 2019
Dwight Dupuch Sep 9, 2019	Alberto Padron Rodriguez Jul 13, 2019	Randall H Browning Mar 28, 2019
Keenen Bullard Sep 8, 2019	Ana Lauren Álvarez Hernández Jul 7, 2019	Roxana Llorens Mar 28, 2019
Oscar Limprich Aug 20, 2019		Jonathan Escobar Mar 25, 2019

IN LOVING

memory

Leandro Lopez
Mar 24, 2019

Andrew Lemon
Jackson
Mar 16, 2019

Osmanny Montano
Mar 10, 2019
Shane Danielle
Tompkins
Jan 20, 2019

Jose Otero
Jan 17, 2019

Linda Marx
Jan 14, 2019

Martaysha Sippio
Dec 28, 2018

Dynette Early
Dec 26, 2018

Delquan Piggat
Dec 16, 2018

Yemil Arguelles
Dec 15, 2018

Corey Davis Jr
Nov 23, 2018

Vickie Boggs
Nov 23, 2018

Waldo Decoste
Nov 20, 2018

Kevin L Willis
Nov 2, 2018

Magaly Benitez
Oct 3, 2018

Marquel Brooks
Sep 29, 2018

Evelio Federico
Gainza
Sep 27, 2018

Vergnio Mondestin
Sep 14, 2018

Netrievae M White
Aug 23, 2018

Tyrone Cobbins
Jul 28, 2018

Marley Jackson
Jul 20, 2018

Junior Catilus
Jun 18, 2018

Dennis Collins
May 26, 2018

Myqueal Fisher
May 16, 2018

Willie Randel
May 16, 2018

Arian Loo
May 5, 2018

Guillermo Martinez
May 5, 2018

Willie Lee "Peanut"
Sabb
May 2, 2018

Emilio Perez
Apr 29, 2018

Al'vonta Shelton
Apr 15, 2018

Alex R Sena
Apr 15, 2018

Kimson Green
Apr 8, 2018

IN LOVING

memory

Rickey Dixon
Apr 8, 2018

James Andrew
Lawrence
Apr 5, 2018

Nyla Jones
Mar 31, 2018

Luis L. Herrera
Kindelan
ar 11, 2018

Alfonso Artice
Mar 4, 2018

Moniqua Kirkland
Feb 23, 2018

Tauraus Holmes
Feb 11, 2018

Priscilla Torres
Feb 10, 2018

Jose Rivero
Feb 6, 2018

Don MacMillan
Jan 28, 2018

Rogelio Castro
Jan 23, 2018

Alfred Alvarez
Jan 22, 2018

Danny Alvarez
Jan 6, 2018

Victor V Carter
Jan 6, 2018

Tony Conway
Jan 3, 2018

Michael Greene
Dec 28, 2017

Jose Velez-Gomez
Dec 27, 2017

Kareem Thomas
Dec 22, 2017

Daniel Tineo
Dec 21, 2017

Shevone Vinson
Dec 17, 2017

Carnell Williams-
Thomas
Dec 15, 2017

Claudel Pinder
Dec 15, 2017

Ricardo Alveiro
Dec 4, 2017

Jason Giles
Dec 1, 2017

Jacques Sylvestre
Nov 16, 2017

Malcolm Nicholas III
Nov 12, 2017

Jorge Leon
Oct 22, 2017

Juliana Quinones
Reinoso
Oct 22, 2017

Victoria Tutson
Sep 26, 2017

Johnny Eugene Brown
Sep 25, 2017

Alfredo Hernandez-
Sierra
Sep 22, 2017

Amberly Hernandez-
Sierra
Sep 22, 2017

IN LOVING

memory

Erika Linarte
Sep 17, 2017

Ralph Carr
Sep 15, 2017

Tyquan "Quan" Ham
Sep 1, 2017

Guillermo Gonzalez
Jr
Aug 6, 2017

Kevin Prince
Jul 29, 2017

Grace Frazier
Jul 28, 2017

Zolonzo K. Smith
Jul 25, 2017

Juan Garcia
Jul 22, 2017

Juwan Downes
Jul 13, 2017

Magdiel Hernandez
Jul 11, 2017

Jackisha Bayard
Jun 30, 2017

Tommy Cooper
Jun 26, 2017

Yasmina Jamal
Jun 22, 2017

Jedediah Scatliffe
Jun 16, 2017

Brian Brown
Jun 14, 2017

Christopher Grant
May 27, 2017

Leonardo Perera
May 27, 2017

Freddy Rijo-Contreras
May 24, 2017

Javonte Jackson
May 23, 2017

Marlin Goodluck
May 23, 2017

Madlin Guardado
May 20, 2017

Yenat Guardado
May 20, 2017

Robert Engleton
May 2, 2017

Robert Henton
Apr 30, 2017

Jasmine Dixon
Apr 23, 2017

Chayvis "Chay" Darice
Reed
Apr 21, 2017

Orlando Miret Jr
Apr 19, 2017

Keith Rolle
Apr 7, 2017

Lester Reid
Apr 3, 2017

Andrew Griffin
Mar 29, 2017

Anthony Gilmore
Mar 26, 2017

Jarvis E. Hill
Mar 26, 2017

Darryl Wayne Smith
Mar 21, 2017

IN LOVING

memory

Gregory Delice
Mar 8, 2017

Bobby Duverny
Feb 22, 2017

Espe Pierre
Feb 22, 2017

Evans Jean
Feb 22, 2017

Norris Cole
Feb 22, 2017

Carlton "Cigar" Fair
Feb 19, 2017

Rosemery Ramirez
Morales
Feb 12, 2017

Jose Manuel Reyes
Feb 4, 2017

Callisto Logan
Jan 31, 2017

Jerald Griffin
Jan 18, 2017

Wilfredo Siam
Jan 12, 2017

Kemorie Wallace
Jan 5, 2017

Ricardo Soler Reyes
Jan 5, 2017

Roland Von Whitaker
Dec 31, 2016

Fernando Duarte
Dec 25, 2016

Alvin Parker
Dec 12, 2016

Keon Crump
Dec 10, 2016

Markeith Nickles
Dec 9, 2016

Jarrett Houston
Dec 5, 2016

Michael Zaldua
Dec 2, 2016

Damien Ramirez
Nov 22, 2016

Howard Watson
Nov 21, 2016

Sonia Williams
Nov 6, 2016

Tavoris Wilson
Nov 5, 2016

Ahmed Jabado
Nov 2, 2016

Bassima Jabado
Nov 2, 2016

Yunia Gomez
Oct 12, 2016

Chadrick G. Davis
Sep 24, 2016

Sir-Ernest Terrell
Williams
Sep 24, 2016

Edward Seymour
Sep 10, 2016

Michael Tito Lorenzo
Sep 10, 2016

VonTavius Sands
Sep 10, 2016

Michael Person
Sep 8, 2016

IN LOVING

memory

Peterson Lamarque
Sep 2, 2016

Jose Anthony Garcia
Aug 30, 2016

Jada Page
Aug 28, 2016

Ricky E. Iglesias
Aug 28, 2016

Isaiah "Zay" Solomon
Aug 27, 2016

Tafari "Fari" West
Aug 27, 2016

Antquinisha Flowers
Aug 25, 2016

Barryson Louis
Aug 25, 2016

Mario Fernandez
Aug 10, 2016

Val Black
Aug 10, 2016

Corey "C.J." Johnson
Jul 31, 2016

Nukeria "Keria" Harris
Jul 31, 2016

Takeeya "KeKe"
Fulton
Jul 31, 2016

Ivy Abigail Torres
Jul 23, 2016

Natasha Bolton
Jul 21, 2016

Jose Gonzalez
Jun 15, 2016

Larry Edwards
Jun 8, 2016

Tremmelle Raymond
Jr
Jun 1, 2016

Lisette Iglesias
May 29, 2016

Wilton Jackson
Apr 24, 2016

Ivis Castro
Apr 10, 2016

Osmand Falls
Apr 5, 2016

Katrina Padgett
Mar 13, 2016

Paul Anderson
Mar 2, 2016

David Goulbarne
Feb 24, 2016

King Carter
Feb 20, 2016

Shalanda Lynn
Feb 15, 2016

Aaron Parrish
Feb 5, 2016

Amiere Castro
Dec 27, 2015

Josmel Herrera
Dec 22, 2015

Shannon Raheem
Dec 20, 2015

Alexus Victoria
Douglas
Dec 2, 2015

Concepccion Loholfftz
Nov 25, 2015

IN LOVING
memory

Johnny Lubin Jr.
Nov 18, 2015

Alfonso Rafael Jr.
Oct 26, 2015

Alfonso Rafael Sr.
Oct 26, 2015

Jose Manuel Ceruto
Sep 16, 2015

Randall Robinson III
Sep 10, 2015

Keith Cox
Aug 25, 2015

Michael Antwan
Jackson
Aug 21, 2015

Wagyns Flerilien
Aug 16, 2015

Juan Meralla
Aug 7, 2015

Miguel Valdes
Jul 26, 2015

Thomas Quass
Jul 4, 2015

Caroline Frye
Jun 23, 2015

Monique Manley
Jun 22, 2015

Schiharia Aila Sai
Kiran
Jun 14, 2015

Joewuan Coles
May 18, 2015

Enrique Fikes
May 5, 2015

Taurus Frazier
May 2, 2015

Jarvis Henderson
Apr 16, 2015

Gretchen LaToye
Miranda
Apr 14, 2015

Sam Salehi
Apr 11, 2015

Joshua Wright
Mar 30, 2015

Marlon Eason
Mar 24, 2015

Richard Hallman
Mar 24, 2015

Willie Warren
Mar 14, 2015

Socorro Delgado
Mar 10, 2015

Ky'Rone Smith
Feb 22, 2015

Reginald Killings
Feb 8, 2015

Aquilina Nino Garcia
Feb 7, 2015

Vinel Lamour
Jan 25, 2015

Lourdes Martinez-
Rodriguez
Jan 13, 2015

Cleveland Lasane
Jan 12, 2015

Alexander Pena
Dec 28, 2014

Frederick Jonell
Gibson
Dec 27, 2014

IN LOVING

memory

Gabriel Figueroa
Dec 26, 2014

James Brown
Dec 25, 2014

Julian Bryant
Dec 14, 2014

Francois Presley
Dec 8, 2014

Pedro Joaquin Uriarte
Nov 30, 2014

Vincent Miller
Nov 15, 2014

Bradley Holt

Nov 13, 2014

Emory Alexander
Sep 14, 2014

Juan Marimon
Sep 7, 2014

Israel Zerquera
Aug 26, 2014

Peter French
Aug 19, 2014

Wilmer Irias
Aug 15, 2014

Rabbi Joseph Raksin
Aug 9, 2014

Jorge Fuentes
Aug 6, 2014

De'Michael Dukes
Jul 21, 2014

Anshamere "Shay"
Cephus
Jul 16, 2014

Kenneth Johnson
Jul 10, 2014

Sandy Celin
Jul 6, 2014

Yanetsy Pastrana
Jul 5, 2014

Kevin Richardson
Jun 24, 2014

Louis Salgar
Jun 24, 2014

Nakiel Jackson
Jun 24, 2014

Justin McAdam
Jun 18, 2014

Kenson Pierre
Jun 18, 2014

Antaun Teasley
Jun 10, 2014

Stanley Blanc
May 25, 2014

Viveka Correa
Apr 29, 2014

Johan Steven Ospina
Apr 14, 2014

Linda Grant
Apr 14, 2014

Wilneka Pennyman
Apr 2, 2014

Herchel Belizaire
Mar 19, 2014

Keimouria Gardner
Mar 19, 2014

Johnny Blidge
Mar 7, 2014

Joefrank Vicente
Feb 2, 2014

Kijuan Byrd
Jun 1, 2012

Sean Taylor
Nov 27, 2007

Albert "DJ Uncle Al"
Moss
Sep 10, 2001

≺≺ The Ripple Effect ≻≻

It is amazing how the death of this little boy has caused a tidal wave of emotions to flow through the Nation like the ripples of a pond after a rock has been dropped into it.

In many ways-King's death was the rock that caused the ripple effect of a social-conscious movement to stop the violence and crimes against children.

Each ripple of a pond represents something. The first ripple closest to the impact represents the lost and life of a child that was so valuable that it created a second ripple. The second ripple was the impact and pain of the family for loosing little King. The pain then duplicated itself, and gave the pain of losing King a voice, that voice began to echo itself, one ripple after another, until that voice could be heard clear up into Heaven where it got the attention of our heavenly Father.

King's death so enraged his Heavenly Father that His anger and Voice sent vibrations through our nation like waves rising up over the ocean. Those waves were just larger ripples of a larger pond that pierced the hearts of a nation that activated a righteous indignation in the hearts of the people in a way that made them rise-up and say-"No more! Not another one!"

King's life, though it appears to be lost, was simply transferred i n t o an energy that is fueling a movement that is going to save countless lives of other children and change the lives of would-be killers all over this world. His death was the most serious mistake that could have ever been made because King's life was connected directly to God's heart.

The senseless killings created a ripple effect of pain, not only for the families but for the world around those that has been murdered. Gun Violence has become a worldwide Crisis. This list goes beyond these that are mentioned. King Carter, Amiere Castro, Marlon Eason, Joewaun Coles, Maurice Harris, Randall Robinson, J o h n n y L u b i n , Sherdavia Jenkins, Travon Martin, Lashonte Jones, can no longer just belong to their parents, but they belong to the community, to our nation, and to us.

Losing our children to senseless gunfire cannot be dismissed and forgotten like the day before yesterday.

The loss of their lives demands change, and the attention of those that have the power to assist in this change. In this movement we are demanding answers and accountability. No child should be able to possess a weapon that was designed for our military. The ripple effect of another child possessing a military style weapon is that, once it is used to kill another human, it reproduces the same ripples of pain, loss, and murder. The pond where these killings are occurring and causing ripples is in our communities. No child should be cut down like a wildebeest while he/she plays in the park, or walks to the store to buy candy.

The ripple effect has a way of calling on justice, and Justice always gets his man. When you take the life or commit a crime against a child.

Justice will always meet out the very same impact to the one that victimized the victim. Just as the first ripple closest to the impact of the victim represents the loss of life and pain- the first ripple of a crime represents the loss of freedom for the criminal, while that ripple duplicates itself and dishes out its own pain to the criminal, it slides right into the third ripple that directly effects the family of the criminal. Even if the family does not suffer physical pain,they must still suffer the loss of their loved-one, which translates into pain, heartache and expenses. Justice makes sure that the ripple effect of a crime goes full circle for the criminal and the victim of the crime. Justice will always victimize the criminal for the sake of the victim of a crime. Justice not served now, is only justice delayed. Justice will never ever not be justice, just as the sun will never not be the sun. No criminal or any person can ever commit a crime against another human without returning the effects of that crime on himself. When we commit crimes against others, or cut short the life of a child, it is no different than turning a loaded gun on yourself and pulling the trigger. We are so intimately connected as humans, that you cannot possibly do something that affects another person and you not be affected yourself.

The ripple effect of our decisions to commit crimes, or fire weapons near children or near innocent bystanders will always circle the effect and impact of your decision to murder, back to you.

You must reap what you sow, you must suffer loss, and your family must suffer loss, you must suffer pain, your family must suffer pain. You must pay; your family has to pay.

Our decision to commit a crime or take a life is to decide to involve our families in our crimes. The crime scene is never the end of a crime;the crime scene is only the first ripple in a sea of troubles that is to come. Our families become ripples in our crimes and the casualties of our decisions to commit those crimes. The ripple effect of our decisions are a perfect zero that encircles everyone that's connected to us, no one is exempt, and everyone has to be impacted as the victim was impacted. It's the law of compensation. There is no escaping the circle of the ripple effect. The ripples of a crime can grow as large as the powers of our government.

Even terrorist in faraway countries that sends an order to the United States to fly airplanes into the World Trade Center could not escape the circle of the ripple effect that he caused.

Though Osama Bin Laden dropped his rock of terrorism clear from the other side of the world he still could not escape the ripple effect that he created by dropping the rock that killed more than 3,000 people and destroying the Twin Towels.

The Ripple Effect is so vast that God from Heaven will summons justice to return the due justice for the victimized to the culprit even if it has to be returned or has to travel clear on the other side of the world. Our military are the ripples of justice. Our local police departments are the ripples of justice. Our federal agencies are the ripples of justice, and when an innocent child is killed, every citizen in this country has to become a ripple of justice.

The children are our future, and it is our supreme duty to protect them.

When we show them love and protect them, those kind acts also create a ripple effect. From those acts of responsibility and love will come a strong nation of young aspiring-inspired leaders who will give back the love and protection that they were shown back to their families, their friends, to the community, and to their country;

When we value the life of humanity and that of children, we are actually dropping the rock that impacts their lives that creates a ripple that initiates their growth and development towards becoming law abiding productive citizens. Their love and confidence in us as their leaders and protectors will continue to duplicate the same kind of ripples that would eventually flood the nation with love, safety and security.

The ripple effect of anything is but an energy that reproduces itself in the exact form of itself, and will return to the creator of the first ripple exactly what was done to cause the ripple. Everything connected to the first ripple will be affected by that ripple no matter how far away you were from the impact.

King Carter's life was an impact into the life of his family. His death was an impact into the lives of those in his community to his friends, throughout the State and this Country. And his energy has been lifted up and carried by the wind that is spreading the ripples of his tragic ending to the four comers of the world. King Carter must not die. If we allow him to die, his energy to cease, or his legacy to travel we concede to the reversed effect of the ripple created by his killers.

And what the reverse ripples of his killers are and will create is a re-creation of King's murder. One murder, and more ripples of a child gone too soon.

King's life was the lesson that we must all learn. King's death is our modem day Rosa Parks that ignited the civil rights movement that changed the entire landscape and racial culture for an entire nation of people. Today our children have become the new targets of a different kind of Jim Crow that's killing them, their dreams and our ability to adequately protect them.

King Carter, Travon Martin, and Heaven Sutton are your sons and daughters.

If we value the lives of these children the way we do freedom then we should construct walls of protection around them as we have our boarders. Our communities should have walls of love around them and the play grounds should be reinforced with security that protects them. The "Office" is an infamous strip club in Miami, Florida that's known for its A-K toting security in its parking lot that protects its employees and money throwing clients. It is safer for a dancer in the parking lot of a night club than it is for a child playing in a park.

There is something undisputedly wrong with that picture. How can we in a free society place more value on a dancer than we do our children. I call this type of behavior a virus. This is a mentality of unconcern that we spread like an influenza. This is life without love. This virus is spread from one mind and one heinous act at a time, throughout our communities, one at a time.

When we become so mis-placed intellectually that we place more security around a business then we do our kids and where they live and play then it can be said that we are now a sick nation. Spreading this virus, that's rippling its way into the homes of parents like Mr. and Mrs. Carter that's ending with them standing on the inside of a funeral home. This should not be so.

Who will have the courage to stand up and be our Rosa Parks? I will! And I will be the rock that's dropped that will start the ripple effect. Mr. and Mrs. Carter will, and all that we are missing is for each and every other individual with a heart, or care and concern, or a child of their own to say, "!will!"

I will stand up against child killings and crimes against children and gun violence.

I will join forces to stop the violence against them. And I will no longer stand by and watch without participating because it was not my child. I will not incarcerate my child in his or her own home, near a playground by keeping him or her in the house because I am afraid that their life will be cut short by a stray bullet.

I am writing this book from a federal prison, where the parents and both grand-mothers of King Carter were invited to see a play that I had written and directed called; (The Ripple Effect and Victim Impact", at Federal Correctional Complex-Medium Coleman, Florida on April 30', 2016. "We would like to contribute a portion of the proceeds of this book to the organizations that support stopping gun violence. "The time to stop the violence has come. If not now-when? If I can initiate an effort to stop the violence from prison, then those of you who are out in society have no excuses. You must never allow me to care more about your sons and daughters than you do. Through me, I have allowed the death of King Carter to affect this entire prison. The ripples of his parent's loss have impacted an entire federal system.

It is ironic that a prisoner is asking society to stand with him on a social issue, when the norm has been to ask society to stand with us on criminal justice, reform and forgiveness.

The death of King Carter is the common denominator that is the cause for us to stand together.

This book is the beginning of our voices from the inside out. Rather than turning our heads away from the problems of society, as rehabilitated, conscious men, we vow to return and take back the same communities we once helped to destroy, and to help eradicate the virus that we once spread.

This book is the pebble that will create an entire tidal wave of ripples that will one day flatten an entire terrain of crimes against our children the way a tsunami flattens an Island standing next to the sea's shore.

May our little King rest in peace, knowing that his life was not lost in vain, may his parents and family find rest and resolve in their moments of pain while knowing that their loss has not only impacted a community, but an entire Bureau of men that are standing with them like soldiers in a time of war.

⤡ The Ripple Effect of a Video Game ⤢

The truth is, if we do not stop gun violence, we are gambling with the reality of one day seeing one of our own children or grandchildren lying in a puddle of blood, lifeless, body riddled with gunshot wounds.

No matter how far away the last accidental shooting was from you and your child, this is a problem that flies by night and can end up in your neighborhood tomorrow. This type of violence is like a disease, if left untreated will never cure itself.

It is more than imperative we realize that we are actually contributing to this problem by allowing our children to be trained like assassins, just as they're trained in the Middle East to become suicide bombers. We are training them to be cold-hearted killers right here in America.

Violent games are the greatest teachers to encourage murder that a child could ever encounter, even more so than using mollies or other mind-altering drugs.

Violent animated video games are the exact way soldiers in the military are trained to kill. The only difference between the two videos used by soldiers and civilians are that one is ca11ed a simulator and marked for "Government Use Only" and the other a game rated for Teens".

Simulators in military are animated training videos that teach an 18-year-old kid how to kill without remorse, which is a teaching that has found its way into our homes and the hands of 18-year-old kids sitting on a couch in our living rooms. Should I be so naive to believe that two 18-year-old kids can be exposed to the same animations to kill and expect a different effect on one because of location and a uniform? Of course not! You'll get the same results: A trained unremorseful killer.

Without realizing it, we are allowing the manufacturers of these games to train our kids' right in our own homes, right before our eyes.

When I was 17-years old, I was running around with some friends that were doing burglaries. One night, about 1:00 AM, we were driving around in the burbs, and one of my friends, recently released from jail, suggested we do a burglary. The most we probablyy expected to get from the burglary was a VCR that we would sell for about $75.00, which would be split 3 ways.

UltimatelyI agreed to do the burglary, but not before I said to the both of them: How can we do a burglary ifthe families were in the house?"

My friend, who'd recently been released from jail, explained that this was the best time to do them because at least we knew that the house was occupied. He also taught me that these particular kinds of burglaries were called "Cat Burglaries", which, he added, carried with them a Life sentence if caught. After everything was explained to me, I said, "Wow! Okay, cool, let's do it."

I sat in the car while my friends did the burglary. The point that I'm making is, when I agreed to do this crime, responding with "Cool" to the knowledge that the crime carried a Life sentence, there was no way that I could have understood the gravity, severity or the impact of what it meant to get a Life sentence at seventeen. Just as a 17 or 18-year old could never fully understand the impact it would have on his family when he gets killed in the streets, or the consequences of killing someone, without ever having had the emotional experience of killing someone realistically, acting instead on what they see and feel in a video game. Such simulators are trick devices that influence kids to kill without knowing the full reality and impact of what it really means to murder someone.

As a community of parents and neighbors who are losing our children to gun violence, we must not be afraid of going after the root cause and reasons of why our children are dying. These violent crimes are not just happening when they occur at the scene of the crime. They began in the minds of these young men long before the actual crime took place. The act of committing murder had been committed repeatedly as part of their training while they sat right across from you playing their video games or listening to their music while popping pills.

We cannot afford to wait until a politician decides to grab our case to use it to attract votes, or for the CEO of a manufacturing company to apologize, because they never will. We must not wait until they decide to accept some responsibility, or for some politician to validate our problem in our communities. Blinded by profits, disconnected by culture and unconcerned by nature, they are emotionally unaffected by our reality and the impact that these games are having on children.

The makers of these games are also trained killers, even if the games are animated. That's why they create and manufacture these types of videos: they get to fulfill all their fantasies of killing without having to pay the consequences of actually doing so. They do this while equating it to a sport, like killing wildlife, calling their kills, "Game". They kill without consequence. It is no less a sport to them, where they kill for profit, when the children kill for real. If it was not so, after reading this book, they would voluntarily pull every violent game from the shelves of all their distributors today.

◄◄ *The Ripple Effect of Leadership and Respect* ►►

Not that I am the only federal prisoner that is highly respected by both staff and other men who are unfortunately in my position. However, to be respected to the degree that I am respected in the federal system is not normal and is therefore considered both noteworthy and extraordinary. To date, I am the only prisoner that I know of that the Bureau has ever authorized to start a movement in an institution. The movement is called: The Reentry and Rehabilitation Movement (RRM, 2015)

With this movement, because of the level of respect that I am given, I am able to call to order more than 400 to 450 men, including every race and nationality, to attend reentry and rehabilitation programs at a drop of a dime.

Due to the love and respect, I get here, with the cooperation of others who are respected by me, I have been able to bring two Hispanic rival gangs together to program in the same room. This is unheard of. This level of respect has enabled me to work with convicted murderers and other well-respected men who have never had respect for life itself. I have the full confidence of knowing how effective I would be out in society, back out in the community, making a difference. Our nation has one of the most valuable resources imaginable at its disposal: Men, who are in federal prison, who are being warehoused like heads of cattle; men, who have been incarcerated for the rest of their lives for non-violent, drug offense, who could be back out in society, cleaning up the streets of their communities. Despite, being a statistic, I have managed to take more than 150 classes/programs, obtain multiple state certifications, earn two degrees, and, as a program facilitator, trained and graduated 80 men per quarter, helping them obtain marketable job skills and trades in Electrical Theory and HVAC. I have studied and learned three other languages and taught some of the most intense classes in the institution. I have also innovated a group, called the Reentry Theatre Group, that performs plays for the institution. I write and direct the plays. These plays are so impactful that they caught the attention of the Obama administration. Also, the Director of the Bureau of Prisons (BOP) ordered the recording of one of the plays, which was converted into a DVD and shown throughout the entire BOP, watched by more than 200,000 prisoners. I have managed to accomplish this despite serving a Life sentence, living in a bathroom with a bunkbed instead of a tub.

There is value in respect and leadership, Respect and

leadership has its own language and understanding. This language is the miscommunication that you see in every cop-related killing involving an African American youth. This language is only understood by men like me, and the youth in our communities.

Many of the men around me toady know that they have a responsibility in what is occurring in our neighborhoods today with the youth. How can they not? Along with the video games, we are the greatest, most influential teachers the youth have ever seen or had. What is great about that statement is if we were able to teach them to be young criminals, then we can re-teach them to be law-abiding citizens.

This is not a fantasy. This is what I do on a daily basis with men who have committed every type of crime imaginable. Over the past 29 years I have taught men how to stand on stage and act in in the plays that I write. I have guided them and influenced them to redirect their lives while changing their complete thought process.

Today these men are not only acting but they are teaching. This play was written in honor of King and of the many families who lost loved ones due to gun violence, in our efforts to stop the violence.

This is the power that comes with love and respect. Love and respect are the first two ripples in the pond of leadership.

This is what our communities are lacking. There is no leadership or respect. And because of the absence of real leadership and respect, the youth are looking to their gang leaders for leadership, love, and respect.

Through sheer love, honor and respect, men like me could affect, impact, and infect communities across America. Because of the respect that we would garner among the youth, with strategies, our children could go back to playing in their front yards and in the local playgrounds and parks.

With the help of media, we can transform our image; we could transform their lives and ultimately our neighborhoods.

This is not a fantasy. This is what I have been doing with men that have committed every crime under the sun for the past 29 years. These results are the ripples of a positive impact that I have been affecting upon this institutional bureau of men every day.

⪻ Who was King Carter? ⪼

King Carter is a six-year-old hero. He is a martyr for change. Though it seems that his life was taken; however, due to our understanding today and efforts to draw from his transition and home-going a full-fledged community makeover, we now realize that his life was neither taken nor lost but given. And because of that, it must not have been given in vain. In many ways, King has been the sacrifice to save many, in the same way Jesus died to save the world.

Every parent in this country owes their respect, empathy and appreciation for the sacrifice made by the Carter family. It may be because of King's martyrdom and every effort that your child gets to live, whether he or she escaped being killed by a stray bullet or at the hands of a cop gone awry.

February 20, 2016 is a day that's worth remembering. That was the day that 6-year-old King Carter was fatally wounded because we fell asleep with him under our watch. Because we have become used to hearing about gun violence. Starting with Columbine, traveling to Arizona, then showing up in a church in South Carolina, before finding its way to Sanford,

Florida, claiming the life of Travon, and ending in Miami, at the Silver Blue Lakes Apartments, ending the life of lil- King.

This has become the norm, so we react in the normal way. Had we not made that mistake, today King would still be alive. To think not would be to think that the Jews of Nazi Germany would escape the Holocaust, only to return to the gas chambers that they know awaits them. Never, ever again will another race of people or a day in time have the opportunity of ever committing another Holocaust upon the Jewish people!

If we, as a community and a nation, had taken that approach at the first sign of gun violence in Columbine, many that have been murdered since, such as 12-year-old Christina Taylor Green, of Arizona, would still be with us.

In America, back in 1987, our legislators saw the need to declare war on non-violent drug offenders, resulting in the incarceration of more than 2 million people. If those resources would have been equally allocated to stop gun violence, there stands a chance that someone that has killed another innocent bystander would have been netted in the round up long before the murder could have occurred. Perhaps the gun that was used to fire the bullet that killed King would have never found its way to the streets of Miami, and into the hand of his killer.

The impact of misallocating those resources have now trickled down into our communities while catching us off guard and asleep just as Osama Bin Laden and his AI Qaeda operatives did on September 11, 2001, that allowed them to murder more than 3,000 innocent people as we slept.

We must now add our young to that list, because we failed to respond to the widespread pandemic of gun violence at its first sign. Instead of attacking this problem, as though we were at war, for the sake of showing favoritism, we labeled the problem as being associated with mental health o r c o n s t i t u t i o n a l s r i g h t and covered up an infested wound with a Band-Aid, leaving the wound oozing with more of what's beneath the Band-Aid. If we do not stop gun violence, the infectious poison of the ripple will always destroy us.

The first killing of an innocent child is just the impact that creates the first ripple. The second ripple is just a reproduction of the first crime and another murder. Those homicides and statistics could only grow in numbers, and as the numbers grow so will the violence.

The Boston bombing was only a larger ripple in the pond and problem of gun violence in this country.

The first time we experience a suicide bombing on American soil; will we realize that we are now experiencing a ripple turned into a tsunami of gun violence, having grown from a single neighborhood shooting of an innocent child, ignored by the system?

King's demise should be the trumpet that sounds the call to stop it. King's death has to and must be just as important as the death of Martin Luther King or Abraham Lincoln. And just as Dr. King's death affected a nation, little King's death must do the same.

His loss of life must carry the same voracity and tenacity, if not more, because the bullet that killed him did not come from the gun of white man, but from one of our own.

Should we stand by idly and wait for the next one? If so, may that blood be on your hands.

King, I leave you with the words of a song by Michael Jackson, which was written just for you:

"You are not alone."

≺≺ Final note from the Author:

The Solution ≻≻

The pebble that could start the ripple effect of the solution to gun violence in the community is a military draft, purposed to clean up our young men who are displaying signs of criminal intent. The military can educate them; training and putting them on enemy lines, letting them exert their anger and frustration toward the terrorist cancer cells currently destroying the world.

Whoa," you say." Are you Crazy?" you ask?

I reply, "I heard that". But what isn't crazy is our need for a community cleansing. And what is also not crazy, the process is already under way. Like it or not, cleaning up our communities is far more important than you not wanting a draft. Besides, if you won't clean up your community to stop the killings, then why complain about someone else doing it?

We cry at funerals, drowning in pain at the agony of losing a loved one, but the thought of the government drafting our young men, educating and cleaning them up, is preposterous to you.

I can totally understand why you would frown on that, because we would feel that we are losing our loved ones by force, to an institution that you feel cares nothing for them. Well what about those families who are losing their sons and daughters by force, like the Carter family, losing their son, and the Jenkins family losing their daughter? These kids were lost at the hand of people who'd be better off in the military, firing their weapons at an enemy that deserves being killed.

For those of you that would frown at the thought of the government coming into our communities, making a major sweep to clean the communities up, no doubt will change your minds once I tell you: I was only kidding about the draft. But what I am not kidding about is the community sweep and clean up.

Mass incarceration is already serving as that process--it is the draft! It's in progress right now. The community cleansing is already in full affect. Those of us that needed to be removed from our communities could not withstand the hand of God, Him removing us for the sake of the community and society, and the families and people we hurt, whether we do it emotionally or physically.

However, the good news is mass incarceration offers a golden opportunity for the government to clean us up and educate us just as the military would do with us as soldiers.

Unfortunately though, for those of us that are caught up in the cleansing process, the government does not prioritize rehabilitation and education above reentry. So, it is a blessing, an exception to the rule, that at FCC Coleman- Medium and F.C.I. Miami, we are fortunate enough to have staff in leadership positions that, sharing in the rehabilitation initiative, possess the unconventional vision to educate us while preparing us for reentry.

Of the 2 million individuals that are incarcerated, if rehabilitating and educating them were the main goal for incarcerating them, the government would be seen through the eyes of the world in a positive way, seeing them as the goose that laid the golden egg, instead of in a negative way, as the country with the highest rate of incarceration in the world.

The solution to cleaning up our communities is already in place, God revealing Himself (yet again) as the best of planners. Even though mass incarceration started out with a racial overtone, GOD CAN TAKE A SITUATION STARTED WITH THE WORST OF INTENTIONS AND BRING ABOUT INSTEAD THE BEST RESULTS.

The story of Joseph, in the book of Genesis, is evidence of this. Joseph was sold into slavery by his brothers because of their envy and jealousy. From there he ended up in prison. Afterward, when Joseph was ultimately reunited with his brothers, he forgave them, saying "What you meant for bad, God has turned into good." (Genesis 50:20)

Likewise, today in the midst of a bad situation, for the 2 million of us that are incarcerated, though our circumstances be peculiar, they're revealing themselves as predestined. In prison, we have the distinct opportunity to clean ourselves up and educate ourselves before returning to our communities, freed not only from prison but too from our old habits, returning us to society as successful, contributing human beings. Through this we're able to give God His glory and praise for outthinking the system, once again turning what was meant for bad into something good.

This suggestion is the first rock that can be dropped into the pond of mass incarceration, the impact from which can cause the first ripple of a mass cleansing. There will never be another time in our lives when we will have an opportunity where 2 million of us are in the same place at the same time, receiving the same education, treatment and cleansing.

The ripple effect from what they did has created one of the greatest opportunities our communities could ever have; through education and rehabilitation, unintentionally, they have given us a chance to clean ourselves up. God's plan, born out of their bad intent.

Mass incarceration is here. The cleansing process began

in 1987. It is what it is. Now let us do our part to come out of it as new men, washed and cleansed as new creations, new sons, new fathers, new husbands, and new citizens in society.

The ripples of mass incarceration must affect those of us that were rounded up for this massive cleansing in a way that our lives and communities will be impacted in such a positive way that we show the world what the mighty hand of God can do. The ripple effect of a mass cleansing is the solution to cleaning up our communities. Through education and rehabilitation, our communities can be safe again.

We need not fear that, once the 2 million of us are cleansed, the violence will continue through others who have not yet been cleansed, because the mandate to clean up our communities and to protect our children is now in the hand of God-Vengeance is mine, says the Lord.

Soon, the word will get out that the massive sweep and round-up continues, and as soon as our young men become tired of being swept up into the system of mass incarceration, they will pronounce their own self-cleansing, begin to do what's right and stop committing violent crimes against children; and eventually, our children will be able to return to the play grounds and parks of their communities to play as children should.

⤙ *Glossary* ⤚

Gun rights **Definition:** The belief that any legislation to curtail the use and sale of firearms is an infringement on Americans' constitutional rights Context: Some groups advocating gun rights believe that firearm-control measures are unnecessary if lawmakers would enforce current laws.

Gun control Definition: The belief that the United States needs stricter firearm laws, including tougher background checks Context: Gun control advocates believe that tougher firearm laws will curb the rise of gun related violence.

Second Amendment Definition: The Second Amendment to the U.S. Constitution states that "A well-regulated Militia, being necessary to the security of a free State, the right of the people to keep and bear Arms, shall not be infringed." Context: The Second Amendment was ratified in 1791

Assault with a deadly weapon- This occurs when the person who attacks uses a harmful object against a person along with a physical attack. This object is considered to be a deadly weapon is it is capable of causing a severe injury to a person or due to its shape and construction, it can kill someone. In each US state, assault with a deadly weapon is considered to be a serious felony.

Background check- Investigating upon a person or an event--this process searches through criminal records, and many others, like financial records, to screen a person in order to ensure security. In regard to gun control, this process of checking helps a registered gun seller to identify whether or not a customer is eligible to purchase a gun from them--if they fail, they might pose as a threat to the safety of the rest of the world.

Defensive gun use-The DGU is the use of a firearm when it is needed in order to protect oneself and also to protect and defend others. There are many differing opinions on what a reason might be to use a gun for self-defense purposes, and such a debate often leads to controversy. In our opinion, however, we believe that firearms are used more so in an attempt to make a person look more intimidating--it is rare that such a weapon is genuinely needed in the purpose of self-defense.

Domestic violence-This type of violence occurs when a partner inflicts emotional and physical abuse on their partner in an attempt to control the other. This is a key topic because domestic violence has been linked to mass shootings. For example, statistics show that abused women are five times more likely to be killed if the person who is abusing them owns a firearm. Many people in abusive relationships find themselves being threatened by their partner who is using the firearm against them--they are often threatened to be either shot or killed.

Federal assault weapons ban- Expired, first signed into law by Bill Clinton. This "crime bill" in the United States regulated the creation and transfer of newly made semi-automatic guns. And ammunition eating devices. After the law was first put into place, only weapons and magazines made after the law was put into place were regulated by law. Any weapon and magazine that was owned prior before the ban were not restricted--the law expired ten years later after it was decided to not renew it.

Firearm-A weapon that is considered to be "small arms"-- these guns might include but are not limited to rifles and pistols. With these types of guns, the bullet that is shot is fired by an explosion inside of the gun caused by gunpowder. Along with that, firearms are both portable weapons and they are also barreled.

Gun control- Any law or policy that keeps tabs and also regulations on the creation, possession and even sale of a firearm. In the United States, there is a huge debate going on between those in favor of gun control laws and those who believe that the Second U.S. Amendment states that they legally have their own personal right to bear arms.

Gun cultures- a group of people's attitudes, feelings, and behavior that these people have towards gun. Around the world, there are very many opinions on gun culture, but the Unites States will remain as one that is most thoroughly studied and discussed.

Gun rights- Often referred to as the right to bear arms; people have their own personal right to defend themselves using an assault weapon. In the United States, the constitution protects the human right to keep and bear arms--this is the common statement used by those who are in support of keeping their gun rights. Along with that, the constitution also states that people have the right to own arms and they also have the right to use them in a militia--clearly, this is a VERY modern way to debate an issue (note the intended sarcasm).

Gun show-A temporary event or gathering in the Unites States in which firearms, accessories and ammunition can be purchased, sold, and even traded. Gun shows are crucial to be discussed because it is here where very many illegal gun transactions are made--this needs to be changed in order to keep our country in line. We cannot have people who are not stable enough mentally to own a gun and most importantly, if this type of weaponry gets into the wrong hands, our country will be doomed, and we will continue to follow on our nation-wide spree of mass shootings.

Mass shooting-Also known as mass murder, this is the intentional and often pre-meditated murder of a large amount of people. An example of times might be the government agents or police officers killing a large number of protestors--also, the Sandy Hook shooting in which 26 lives were lost as a result is another example.

Magazine-In firearms, this is a storage and feeding device for ammunition that usually is attached to an automatic firearm or it can be inside of one; the magazines are often detachable, however. There is a ban in the United States on high-capacity magazines, this was included in 1994's Assault Weapons Ban.

National Firearms Act-Also known as the NFA--this is a United States Act of Congress that puts an inland tax on the creation and transfer of many different firearms (but not all).

Non-criminal gun violence-This type of gun violence may occur when there is an accidental injury or death inflicted upon a person due to the use of a gun. Of course, as these types of violent crimes are not as common as ones that are in fact criminal, they are still very real, and they appear to be a pressing concern for the United States.

NRA-Also known as the National Rifle Association of America. This American organization is aimed to protect the United States constitution and most specifically, their efforts are posed mainly at keeping the right to bear and keep arms alive for all US citizens. Personally, we criticize this group for the actions that they have taken to get their message across--they are bringing military style weaponry into businesses as a way to prevent the creation of gun laws. Unfortunately, this group seems to think that gun control advocates are out to get them, when in reality, we are trying to protect our families and children from the disturbing number of shootings that have been occurring lately--this group of people shows nothing but selfishness.

Citations:

"JURIST - Legal Dictionaries." JURIST - Legal Dictionaries. N.p., n.d. Web. 4 June 2014. <http://jurist.law.pitt.edu/dictionary.htm>.

Cambridge Dictionaries Online!." Cambridge Free English Dictionary and Thesaurus. N.p., n.d. Web. 4 June 2014. <http://dictionary.cambridge.org/us/>.

≪ *A special thanks* ≫

A special thanks to the Executive Staff for their support; F.C.I Miami, Warden Sylvester Jenkins, A.W. Broton, Mr. Manuel Ocasis, Warden, Mr. Manuel Cole, Associate Warden, Ms. Rapunzel Stephens-Clements, Mr. Gary Lee, A Unit Manager, To the Reentry Theater Group and to the Bureau of Prisons.

≺≺ About the Author ≻≻

Wayne Anderson is a federal prisoner incarcerated since September 13, 1993. He is serving a life sentence for a nonviolent drug offense. Mr. Anderson worked as clerk and classroom instructor in the Vocational Training and Education Department at Federal Correctional Complex Coleman- Medium for almost five years.

Prior to working as an educational clerk, Wayne worked for the Federal Prison Industries, Inc. (UNICOR) at the United States Penitentiary Atlanta as an Accountant technician, overseeing an entire warehouse of merchandise known as SSTI.

Wayne is certified in a variety of areas, such as computer programs. He is certified in Microsoft Excel, Microsoft Word, PowerPoint, Access, as well as System Application Production (SAP), commonly referred to as *Millennium,* an official record keeping and integrated manufacturing, accounting software package and management information system.

Wayne has created and innovated programs for the bureau of Prisons; such a fathers Rebuilding Bridges program; Mothers Rebuilding Bridges for the women Camp; The first ever Spanish Threshold class (a spiritual based program for

Hispanics); the Reentry and Rehabilitation Movement; He co-authored the curriculum for The Bridge to Reentry; he has also served as a mentor in the Skills program where he was paired up with mentally challenged inmates as a Mental Health Companion.

Wayne is the innovator for one of the most highly recognized program s in the Bureau of Prisons called The Reentry Theatre Group. This group are used to perform the plays that are written by Wayne.

"Has earned a degree in business with honors from Ashworth College, and is currently working on his Bachelors of Arts Degree from Adams State University.

Wayne has also learned to speak Spanish, while also studying Portuguese, and the Italian language.

Wayne is a humble spirit, who lives by Christian principles. He prides himself with knowing that today he is truly a rehabilitated human being who serves God and humanity with a passion.

"True service i s when serving o t h e r s become a habit."

You cannot be who you were, and who you have become at the same time.

_____ ***Wayne Anderson***

GUNS ARE NOT THE SOLUTION

Let's stop the VIOLENCE.

ALL LIVES MATTER

#TREOGV

#THERIPPLEEFFECTOFGUNVIOLENCE